COLLECTIVE BARGAINING SIMULATED

Computerized and Noncomputerized Formats

FOURTH EDITION

Jerald R. Smith
Florida Atlantic University

Michael R. Carrell
University of Nebraska
Omaha

Peggy A. Golden
Florida Atlantic University

Prentice Hall, Upper Saddle River, NJ 07458

Library of Congress Cataloging-in-Publication Data

Smith, Jerald R.
    Collective bargaining simulated: computerized and noncomputerized formats /
Jerald R. Smith, Michael R. Carrell, Peggy A. Golden—4th ed.
        p.   cm.
    ISBN 0-13-521998-1 (pbk.)
    1. Collective bargaining—United States. I. Carrell, Michael R.
II. Golden, Peggy A. III. Title
HD6971.5S65 1996   95.25245
331.89—dc20   CIP

Acquisitions Editor: Natalie Anderson
Associate Editor: Lisamarie Brassini
Editor-in-Chief: Jim Boyd
Production Editor: Louise Rothman
Buyer: Ken Clinton
Marketing Manager: Susan McLaughlin

© 1996 by Prentice-Hall, Inc.
A Simon & Schuster Company
Upper Saddle River, New Jersey 07458

Type: CG Times 11.8

Printed in the United States of America

10 9 8 7 6 5

ISBN 0-13-521998-1

PRENTICE-HALL INTERNATIONAL (UK) LIMITED, *London*
PRENTICE-HALL OF AUSTRALIA PTY. LIMITED, *Sydney*
PRENTICE-HALL CANADA INC., *Toronto*
PRENTICE-HALL HISPANOAMERICANA, S.A., *Mexico*
PRENTICE-HALL OF INDIA PRIVATE LIMITED, *New Delhi*
PRENTICE-HALL OF JAPAN, INC., *Tokyo*
SIMON & SCHUSTER ASIA PTE, LTD., *Singapore*
EDITORA PRENTICE-HALL DO BRASIL, LTDA., *Rio de Janeiro*

The authors would like to thank the schools that adopted past editions of <u>Collective Bargaining Simulated</u> for their helpful comments and suggestions.

Antelope Valley College
Auburn University
Auburn University, Montgomery
Augusta College
Baylor University
Bellarmine College
Bellevue University
Bently College
Blackhawk Technical Institute
Black Hills State College
Bunker Hill Community College
Cabrini College
California State University,
  Bakersfield
California State University, Chico
California State University,
  Los Angeles
Carroll College
Central Washington University
Central Michigan University
Central Texas University
City College, Seattle
Claremont Graduate School
Clayton State College
Clearwater Christian College
Cleveland State University
Columbia College
Concord College
Cornell University
Corpus Christi State University
Creighton University
DePaul University
Dina Ferguson
East Carolina University
Eastern College
Eastern Illinois University
Eastern Kentucky University
Elizabeth City State University
Embry Riddle Aero University
Essex Community College
Florida International University

Fort Hayes State University
Friends University
Gerogetown University
Georgia College at Milledgeville
Georgia Institute of Technology
Glassboro State College
Golden Gate University
Grand Valley State University
Gwynedd-Mercy College
Houston, University of
Howard University
Indiana University, Kokomo
Illinois Wesleyan University
Jackson Business Institute
Johns Hopkins University
Kennesaw College
Kent State University
Lafayette College
Lakeshore VTAE District
Lamar University
Lehigh University
Lewis & Clark State College
Longview Community College
Macon Junior College
Mary Washington College
McKendree College
Miami University
Morehead State University
Muskegon Community College
National University, San Diego
Nazareth College of Rochester
Neumann College
Niagara University
Norfolk State University
Northeast Wisconsin Tech
Northeastern Oklahoma A & M
  College
North Georgia College
North Harris City College
North Texas State University
Northern Virginia CC Annadale

Ohio Dominican College
Ohio University
Oklahoma Christian College
Oklahoma State University
Oklahoma State University of
Agriculture and Applied Science
Old Dominion University
Our Lady of the Lake University
  of San Antonio
Pennsylvania State University
Philadelphia State College of Textiles &
  Science
Plymouth State College of the University
  of New Hampshire
Purdue University, Calumet
Ramapo College of New Jersey
Regents College
Robert Morris College
Rockhurst College
Saint Johns University
Saint Josephs University
Saint Louis Community College
  at Meramec
Saint Thomas University
Salem State College
San Jose State University
Santa Monica College
Shawnee State Community College
South Dakota State University
Southeastern Massachusetts University
Southern Technical Institute
Spalding University
Springfield College
Stetson University
SUNY College at Fredonia
SUNY College at Oswego
SUNY College at Utica
Syracuse University
Texas A & M University
Thomas College
Troy State University
University of Akron
University of Alaska, Juneau
University of Arizona
University of Baltimore

University of Bridgeport
University of Central Arkansas
University of Central Florida
University of Cincinnati
University of Colorado,
  Colorado Springs
University of Georgia
University of Iowa
University of Kansas
University of La Verne
University of Louisville
University of Missouri
University of New Orleans
University of Oregon
University of Saint Thomas
University of South Florida
University of Southern Mississippi
University of Southwestern Louisiana
University of Texas, San Antonio
University of Virginia
University of Wisconsin-La Crosse
University of Wisconsin-Oshkosh
Vincennes University
Walla Walla College
Washington State University
Wentworth Institute of Technology
West Chester University of
  Pennsylvania
Western Carolina University
Western Connecticut State University
Western Michigan University
Western New England College
West Virginia State College
West Virginia University
Wichita State University
Willmar Community College
Wilson College
Winthrop College
Wright State University

TABLE OF CONTENTS

FOREWORD

The process of collective bargaining is exciting and dynamic. It can require the knowledge of a specialized surgeon, the patience of a little league coach, the fortitude of a military general, the social skills of a PTA president, and much more. Few fields require as great a degree of legal expertise, quantitative skills, and human relations ability. The developers of this simulation believe, based on years of teaching and negotiation, that the traditional lecture and case approach to teaching collective bargaining can be greatly enhanced by giving students this "hands-on" experience in contract negotiations.

ARCO, a major metals corporation, gave us permission to use one of their labor agreements as the current to be re-negotiated in this simulation. Only the names were changed (and a few numbers) to guarantee that the basic contract provides students with a "real world" experience. The descriptions of the company, union, and past labor management relations were based on interviews with company and union officials. The student, however, is not restrained to the limits of this particular company since new negotiations always provide the opportunity for innovation and creativity.

The simulation has been classroom tested by thousands of students and is designed for use in seminars, training programs, and college level instruction. The simulation can be utilized by itself, in a one day seminar for example, or together with a conventional textbook over a period of weeks. It is most appropriate for undergraduate or graduate courses in collective bargaining, labor relations, personnel administration, labor economics, labor law, or wage and salary administration. It has also been utilized in the traditional business policy capstone course.

We believe that we have added an exciting new dimension to the usual collective bargaining simulation by providing a computer program which will (a) cost-out economic items such as proposed wage increases, and/or (b) directly negotiate a contract with the student, with the computer representing the union. This program provides the instructor with an almost unlimited number of alternative methods of using the simulation, including letting each student directly and individually negotiate a new agreement outside the classroom or negotiate in groups.

If we can assist you in your use of the simulation, please do not hesitate to contact us. Contact Dr. Carrell for student manual clarifications or suggested classroom use and Dr. Smith or Dr. Golden concerning the computer program. This fourth edition is quite similar to the third but incorporates changes suggested by third edition users and new contract issues.

Jerald R. Smith
Graduate School of Business
Florida Atlantic University
Ft. Lauderdale, FL 33301

Michael R. Carrell
College of Business Adm
University of Nebraska, Omaha
Omaha, NE 68182

Peggy A. Golden
College of Business
Florida Atlantic University
Ft. Lauderdale, FL 33301

HOW TO USE THIS SIMULATION

The simulation is designed to be used by only one participant or an entire class. It can be utilized in as short a period of time as two hours reading time followed by two hours negotiating or it can take as long as four weeks--if several participants negotiate for each side and all the forms provided in this booklet are fully utilized. This great degree of flexibility is achieved by taking advantage of computerized <u>costing</u> and <u>negotiation programs</u>. However, it is important to remember that the entire simulation can be utilized <u>without</u> the computerized programs if so desired.

The simulation primarily involves five phases:

PHASE I: <u>PREPARATION</u>

     a. review of current agreement

     b. familiarization of other booklet material--the Company, the Union, etc.

     c. <u>Choice of Simulation Format</u>:

          1. Each participant can negotiate individually with the computer. (Using both the costing and negotiation programs.)

          2. Teams of participants can negotiate against the computer. (Using both the costing and negotiation programs.)

          3. Teams of participants can negotiate against each other. (Using only the costing program.)

          4. Teams of participants can negotiate against each other (without using either computer program.)

PHASE II: <u>PRE-BARGAINING STRATEGY</u>

Teams should determine individual roles and discuss negotiation strategy. Initial economic and non-economic priorities are then finalized. (Forms A, B, C or A, L, M)

PHASE III: <u>OPENING NEGOTIATION SESSION</u>

     a. Ground rules for negotiation need to be agreed upon <u>before</u> initial demands are exchanged. (Form D)

     b. Initial demands should be exchanged and explained. (Forms E or N)

c. Future negotiation sessions (day, time, and location need to be determined).

PHASE IV: ADDITIONAL NEGOTIATION SESSIONS

a. Proposals and counter-proposals of economic and non-economic items are exchanged until both sides reach agreement on all items. (Form F)

b. Each team, in the non-computerized format, may choose to agree to and "sign and date" individual items as they are agreed to, or may wait until the final contract is negotiated. (Form G)

PHASE V: SIMULATION REVIEW

a. Teams may conduct a performance audit on another team's negotiations. (Form I)

b. Team members should appraise fellow teammates' contribution. (Form J)

c. Each participant should evaluate the simulation. (Form K)

THE COMPANY: OHIO METALS

In 1947 Dennis and Mike Johnson decided that they could make a living from what had been a part-time hobby: producing metal parts for automobiles, electrical components, industrial machinery, etc. They had grown up in Cincinnati, Ohio, and had always enjoyed "tinkering" with car engines and other motors. During the war several small businessmen had learned of their ability to repair almost any motor or mechanical device quickly and cheaply. Since new engines or parts were hard to find, the young men quickly built up a trade working out of their garage. In 1949 they decided more space was needed, so a larger building was constructed behind Dennis' house, and their first employee, Dennis' wife Nancy, was hired to keep the books. In 1950 the brothers decided to call themselves "Ohio Metals" and signed a contract with General Motors to perform repair work on operating equipment at the Cincinnati assembly plant. Their first brush with organized labor occurred at this time when GM's union objected to the brothers performing any work which could be performed by union labor--all parties agreed that Ohio Metals would only perform work not normally performed by union members.

After several years of moderate success, the Johnson brothers were presented with a major decision in 1956. That year two local firms which had contracted with them periodically offered them large contracts to produce sheet metal parts which the firms had previously bought from a Cleveland supplier. Impressed with Ohio Metals' consistent quality and low prices, the firms asked the Johnsons to consider supplying them with the parts on a permanent basis. To accept the contract would mean a major expansion of facilities and equipment--as well as expanding their workforce of 26. The Johnsons decided that the diversification and expansion presented them new and exciting challenges they could not afford to miss. By 1961 they had built an entirely new facility, expanded to 300 employees, and found that 70% of their business was in the production of sheet metals and associated products. It was that year in which the employees organized Local 56. The process was peaceful and quickly completed.

The firm continued to grow rapidly in both primary areas--sheet metals and motor parts and service. In 1965 a major expansion was begun as a means of meeting increased demand. The Johnson brothers had insured that quality and timely completion of orders was continued during the company's growth. This sometimes resulted in the loss of additional business. The 1965 expansion was achieved by incorporating under the name of Ohio Metals, Inc., with an issuance of 10,000 shares of stock. The Johnson brothers each kept 2,600 shares and the remainder was sold over the counter. The firm continued to gradually grow in all respects.

By 1973 over 1,000 people were employed, and the Johnsons were multi-millionaires. However, in that year two events occurred which drastically changed the course of the firm's history. First, the Arab oil embargo began a chain of events which would affect virtually all of the firm's major clients. Within ten years 60% of the firms which accounted for their 1973 sales would be out of business. Many of those firms were customers for ten years or longer. At the same time, new customers became harder to recruit. The second major event of 1973 was the death of Dennis Johnson. Killed by a drunk driver, his death triggered the end of the Johnson family's management of the firm. Mike Johnson, Nancy Johnson and three other family members

3

retired within three years. The heirs of Dennis Johnson sold much of their company stock which ended the family's majority holding.

From 1974 to the mid 1980s, Ohio Metals suffered from the economic recession in the auto related industry. Under the leadership of T. J. Barry, who replaced Dennis Johnson, the firm was able to maintain a reputation for quality and the completion of orders on time. However, the market as a whole continued to decline, and by 1978 the workforce had been depleted to 491. By gradual product expansion as well as some ingenious successful government contract bidding by Barry, Ohio Metals survived the 70's recession better than most.

In the 1980's employment rebounded to about 700, and sales more than doubled. It is generally believed that if Barry and the younger executives he brought with him had not come aboard when they did things might not have been nearly as good today. The Johnsons simply had become relaxed and less energetic in their last years. They had not developed the aggressive approach to marketing and production problems. However, no one has forgotten that the company's reputation, which was built by the Johnsons, was largely responsible for its ability to maintain and attract new customers.

Today the metals industry in Ohio and nearby states has experienced some recent new growth. Some of the "rust belt" plants which closed in the 70s or early 80s have reopened under new ownership. In general, however, these new operations are smaller, pay lower wages, and are very cost conscious. It is clear that Ohio Metals today is in a very competitive market which experiences economic swings as the U.S. auto industry rises or falls. A relatively small operation, Ohio Metals can only hope to retain its market share if it continues to make deliveries on time and maintain its high quality. The firm's financial condition is shown on the following page.

As negotiations begin, both management and employees remain "cautiously optimistic" about the future. Both feel that while the company is sound, it must continue to produce high quality products and deliver them "just-in-time" because more nonunion and international competitors appear each year.

OHIO METALS COMPANY, INC.
CONFIDENTIAL FINANCIAL INFORMATION
(rounded to nearest 000's)

INCOME AND EXPENSE STATEMENT	*2003* 12-30-~~1995~~	*2002* 12-30-~~1994~~	*2001* 12-30-~~1993~~
Sales	*50,029,000* $ ~~49,324,000~~	*44,590,000* 39,590,000	*38,060,000* 33,060,000
Production Costs Including Materials	*22,150,000* - ~~23,100,000~~	*22,075,000* - 20,075,000	*19,400,000* - 17,400,000
Production Wages	- ~~16,965,000~~ *21,206,000*	- ~~12,725,000~~ *15,725,000*	- 10,650,000 *13,650,000*
Gross Profit	~~9,259,000~~ *6mill* *7,472,750*	~~6,790,000~~ *6,790,000*	5,010,000
Administrative and Selling Costs	- *2*,800,000	*2*,600,000	*1,420,000* ~~2,410,000~~
Overhead	- ~~1,550,000~~ *756,000*	~~1,150,000~~ *600,000*	~~950,000~~ *540,000*
Net Profit Before Taxes	*4,916,750* 4,909,000	*4,590,000* ~~3,040,000~~	1,650,000 *3,050,000*
Income Tax	*-1,020,862* 2,020,000	*-1,040,000* ~~1,240,000~~	~~660,000~~ *1,000,000*
Profit After Tax	*3895888* 2,889,000	*3,550,000* ~~1,800,000~~	~~990,000~~ *1,900,000*
Dividends Paid	- *600,000*	- ~~400,000~~ *300,000*	~~0~~ *-200,000*
Net Profits	*3,295,888* ~~2,489,000~~	*3,250,000* 1,700,000	~~990,000~~ *1,770,000* = *1.48mill*
Cash and Other Liquid Assets	523,200	*1*27,300	*1*40,700

Note: The production manager has completed an equipment needs analysis and has concluded the company will need to invest approximately $6,400,000 on new equipment within the next three years. The firm currently has $6,500,000 of long-term debt.

INDUSTRY INFORMATION:

Avg. One Year Wage Increase Last Year	2.0%
Productivity Increase	2.5%
Local Unemployment	6.9%
Cost of Living Increase Last Year	2.0%

THE UNION: LOCAL 56

Local 56 of the Primary and Sheet Metals Workers of America, AFL-CIO, was certified as the exclusive bargaining agent for Ohio Metals, Inc., of Cincinnati, Ohio, in 1961. The certification election came after little company resistance to unionization. In fact from the beginning, union and management leaders have exhibited positive, friendly relations with few exceptions. Since its certification, the union has brought only twelve grievances to the point of binding arbitration, and not one production day has been lost due to a strike, nor has even one delivery date been affected. Much of the good labor relations of the past is credited to the positive attitude of the Johnsons and Barry. However, they, like most, would credit Brooks Wilson, President of Local 56 from 1971 to the present, with the successful working relationships of labor and management. Wilson, together with Janice Barnes, the business agent, and James Knight, have negotiated all of the recent collective bargaining agreements between Ohio Metals, Inc., and Local 56.

Wilson has always advocated multi-year agreements which, according to him, provide for a "stable labor-management partnership with a long-run perspective." Most past agreements were for a period of three years. The current agreement is for one year, however, because the last round of negotiations were strained. During the last contract the union did come very close to an economic strike when, after six months of negotiations, an agreement had not been reached. In previous negotiations the process had never taken longer than two months, and only once had the members worked under a continuance of the old contract on a day-to-day basis. A key issue in the last contract negotiations was the lack of a subcontracting limitation clause--a demand finally dropped by the union. The union also believed management was not willing to "share the new prosperity."

In recent years some union members have become restless. Once a leader in wages and benefits in the Cincinnati area, both labor and management had resisted significant increases during the last three negotiating sessions in order that the company maintain its competitive position and minimize layoffs. However, most employees feel that the company has now "turned the corner" and that it is time to regain ground lost to inflation and the recession. They also note that since Barry became President they have not been able to negotiate a "generous" contract. However, the members are quite aware that many unions in their industry have been forced into "concession" or "give back" bargaining which to date has been successfully avoided by Local 56. They also realize that thousands of jobs similar to theirs have been lost due to layoffs and plant closings.

Most union members believe management's claim that a substantial wage increase could cause the company to lose its competitive position. However, they also believe that the company's profits of recent years have exceeded expectations, and while Barry has given large bonuses to top managers, he has not shared this prosperity with union members. Thus, the union negotiators know they must achieve economic gains at the table to keep their membership from voting to strike. However, management continues to adamantly claim that their market is quite volatile and last year's profits do not guarantee the ability to pay higher wages in the future.

6

At the same time, members are tired of averaging 8 hours of overtime per week. Thus they would like the overtime provision to be changed to provide that all overtime would be voluntary. The expansion in the sheet metal industry in recent years has caused a substantial need for additional production, yet management has resisted hiring more employees when overtime can provide the needed labor.

It has been recently rumored that management has considered sub-contracting work which could cause layoffs of 20% of the union workers, or reduce almost all scheduled overtime in several areas combined with layoffs in others. The rumor has caused considerable unrest in the union.

A major irritant to workers is the new random drug testing program. Originally presented as a safety program due to a high rate of accidents, many union members now believe testing without probable cause is unnecessary and an invasion of their privacy.

UNION-MANAGEMENT RELATIONS

Currently, the atmosphere between labor and management is positive, but tense--more so than anyone can remember. The union members firmly believe they had to "bite the bullet" for the last seven years and three negotiations. Rumors are strong that the employees will strike if necessary, but they do not want to break their "no-strike" tradition and possibly endanger the company. Management claims that the economic recovery of the firm is fragile and that a large wage and price increase would hurt their competitiveness. Also a strike could seriously impair the firm's ability to maintain its record of completing orders on time. Barry would like to return to a three-year agreement which would make it easier to bid on contracts. He has told Wilson that the union must be willing to give back longevity pay for any substantial economic gains, because he prefers "pay for performance." He is open to a profit-sharing proposal, but insists on retaining the right to subcontract work.

The current contract expires within the next few weeks. In preparation for negotiations, Wilson, as he always has done in the past, surveys his members and provides a copy of the results to management. He is quite serious about using the results to guide him during negotiations. The results of the survey (96% response) are listed on page 9. (Each employee listed in rank order their top five concerns.) However, Wilson also knows that job security is important to his members who have suffered through several layoffs and reduced work weeks. Most important, he knows that his members have total confidence in his leadership.

Barry has conferred with his staff and believes management can ill afford a strike which would interrupt contracts currently under production. He would like to be fair to the workers who have generally been loyal to the company, but he fears increased nonunion and international competition, as well as a possible economic downturn.

SURVEY OF EMPLOYEE PREFERENCES

Item	% listed	% listed #1	
Economic			
Wage increase	89	44	1
Pension benefit increase	70	14	5
Fully paid health insurance	67	14	5
Profit-sharing plan	65	13	6
Higher shift differential	31	4	9
Paid funeral leave	29	0	—
Additional paid holidays	25	4	9
Additional vacation leave	22	4	9
Pension increase	20	0	—
Higher clothing allowance	21	0	—
Longevity pay increase	11	3	10
Non-economic			
No sub-contracting	65	23	3
Voluntary overtime	54	25	2
No random drug testing	44	15	4
No part-time employees	34	15	4
Job posting program	32	12	7
Three-year contract	29	10	8
Better cafeteria food	14	0	—

9

NON-ECONOMIC ISSUES

The listing below represents the various positions each side could take on each non-economic item listed on the previous page.

Item   Alternative

1. Job Posting:
   1. All bargaining unit jobs posted and filled through seniority as the sole criteria.
   2. All bargaining unit jobs posted and filled through seniority of those qualified.
   3. All bargaining unit jobs posted and filled with the most senior of those qualified within the department.
   4. All bargaining unit jobs filled according to seniority and ability.

2. Overtime:
   1. Overtime assigned by seniority within job classification and on a voluntary basis only.
   2. Overtime assigned by seniority within job classification and on a voluntary plant-wide basis (e.g. someone outside the job classification could bid on the overtime).
   3. Overtime assigned by management under current Article XXI, but after an employee accumulates 10 hours/week of overtime, it will be assigned on a voluntary basis.
   4. Keep Article XXI - overtime assigned by management.

3. Employee Drug Testing:
   1. Drug testing only for probable cause.
   2. Drug testing for probable cause or after an accident or incident of theft.
   3. Drug testing for probable cause, after an accident or incident of theft, and in the department with a high rate of OSHA violations (on a random basis).
   4. Drug testing of all employees on a random basis, including managers (the current program).

4. Part-time Employees:
   1. Management hires part-time employees with the approval of the union.
   2. Management hires part-time employees; they must join the union immediately.
   3. Management hires part-time employees; they must join union within 3 months.
   4. No change in part-time policy (Management hires whenever needed. Employee does not have to join union unless retained for over 6 months and then must pay union dues.

5. Sub-contracting:
    1. No sub-contracting of any currently performed work.
    2. No sub-contracting without prior union approval.
    3. Sub-contracting on an emergency or limited-time basis.
    keep ← 4. Sub-contracting only when determined by management as necessary to meet contractual demands.

6. Cafeteria Food: *union can have* —
    1. Union to select cafeteria operator.
    2. Union and management to jointly select cafeteria operator.
    3. Union to have 45% representation on cafeteria committee.
    4. Company to control cafeteria as it is now doing.

7. Length of contract:
    1. One year.
    2. Three-year contract with wage re-opener.
    — 3. Three-year contract with wage re-opener and zipper clause.
    — 4. Three-year contract with zipper clause.

AGREEMENT
BETWEEN

**The Ohio Metals, Inc., Company
And
The Primary and Sheet Metal
Workers of America
AFL-CIO**

Cincinnati, Ohio

INDEX

PREAMBLE

This Agreement is entered into this 1st day of June, 1993, between the Ohio Metals, Inc. Company, Cincinnati, Ohio, hereinafter referred to as the "Company," and the Primary and Sheet Metal Workers of America, AFL-CIO, hereinafter referred to as the "Union."

ARTICLE I
Intent and Purpose

It is the desire of the Company and the Union to promote mutual cooperation and harmony and to formulate rules for their guidance to accomplish these ends. Therefore, for the purpose of establishing rates of pay, hours of work, application of seniority rights, and general working conditions of employment, the Company and the Union agree to the following provisions.

ARTICLE II
Recognition

SECTION 1. The Company recognizes the Union as the exclusive collective bargaining agent for all its production and maintenance employees, located at its plant in Cincinnati, Ohio. This group does not include official clerical, plant protection, professional or technical employees or supervisors as that term is defined in the National Labor Relations Act.

SECTION 2. The Union agrees that neither it nor any of its officers or members will intimidate or coerce any employee of the Company; the Company will not interfere with or discriminate against any members or officers of the Union on account of their activities for and on behalf of the Union.

SECTION 3. There shall be a probationary period of ninety (90) working days to allow the Company to determine the fitness and adaptability of a new employee to do the work required and whether it desires to retain such employee, during which time the new employee shall accumulate no seniority and may be discharged without recourse to the grievance procedure. If, however, such employee is retained beyond the probationary period, his seniority shall date from the date of hire.

ARTICLE III
Management

The management of the plant and the direction of its working force is vested exclusively in the Company. These functions are broad in nature and include such things as the right to schedule work and shift starting and stopping times, to schedule overtime, and to contract out work. It also has the right to hire and to discharge for just cause, to transfer or lay off because of work load distribution or lack of work. In the fulfillment of these functions the Company agrees not to violate the following Articles or the intent and purpose of this Agreement, or to discriminate against any member of the Union.

It is the continuing policy and recognized obligation of the Company and the Union that the provisions of this Agreement shall be applied fairly and in accordance with those federal and state employment laws relating to race, color, sex, religious creed, age, national origin, handicap, disabled veterans and Veterans of the Vietnam Era.

All masculine pronouns, titles, and references in this agreement include the feminine gender.

ARTICLE IV
Union Shop and Check-Off

SECTION 1. Except as provided in Section 2 of this Article, all employees who are members of the Union shall be required to maintain their membership in good standing, during the life of this Agreement, in the Union by paying the periodic dues and initiation fees uniformly required of all Union members as provided for in the Union Constitution, as a condition of continued employment. Except as provided in Section 2 of this Article, all other employees and newly hired employees shall join the Union upon the completion of their ninetieth (90th) working day from the most recent date of hire, or thirty (30) days after the execution of this Agreement, whichever is later, and shall thereafter maintain their membership in good standing in the Union, during the life of the Agreement, by paying the periodic dues and initiation fees uniformly required of all Union members, as a condition of continued employment.

SECTION 2. Any employee or newly hired employee who, because of good faith membership in a church or religious faith which holds as one of its tenants or beliefs that he may not join or become a member of the Union, need not comply with the provisions of Section 1 of this Article IV but shall, as a condition of employment, after the ninetieth (90) working day from the most recent date of hire or thirty (30) days after execution of this Agreement, whichever is later, contribute a service fee to the Union in accordance with the procedures for payment and check-off, as hereinafter provided in this Article, equal to dues required of members, which service fee shall be in full compensation to the Union for acting as his agent in matters covered by this Agreement.

SECTION 3. The Company shall deduct from the first full pay period of each month the Union dues for the preceding month, assessments and initiation fees, each as designated by the International Treasurer of the Union, and remit same to the International Treasurer.

Sums to be remitted to the International Treasurer shall be mailed from Sugarcreek, Ohio, or from such other accounting office convenient to the Company, together with information as to the breakdown between dues, initiation fees and assessments.

ARTICLE V
Hours of Work

SECTION 1. This Article V is intended to define the normal hours of work and how they shall be scheduled and paid. It is not to be construed as a guarantee of hours of work per day, or of days of work per week.

SECTION 2. A day is a twenty-four hour period, commencing with the start of the employee's shift.

A week is seven (7) twenty-four (24) hour periods, commencing with the start of the employee's shift on Monday of each week.

A normal work day is eight (8) consecutive hours of work in a twenty-four (24) hour day, broken only by the established lunch period.

A normal work week is five (5) consecutive work days, Monday through Friday. It is understood that there will be no pyramiding of overtime.

SECTION 3. The normal starting time for day shift employees shall be 7:00 a.m. and for night shift employees, 4:00 p.m. The Company may, at its discretion, change the normal shift starting and stopping times. Changes in the normal shift starting

and stopping times shall be posted not later than the prior Thursday and be effective with the commencement of work on Monday. Notice of these changes will be given to the Union President or his designated representative prior to this posting.

ARTICLE VI
Reporting and Call-In Pay

SECTION 1. When an employee is recalled for emergency or overtime work after completing a shift and leaving the premises for the day, he will be paid a minimum of four (4) clock card hours. If called in for such work on a Saturday or Sunday without having been notified on the previous Friday, he will be paid a minimum of four (4) clock card hours. In either instance, the appropriate overtime premium will be payable on the specified hours.

The Company reserves the right to utilize the employee's time for the full amount of hours for which he will be paid when called in to work as outlined above.

SECTION 2. Any employee reporting for work without having been properly notified by the Company that there will be no work, shall be paid a minimum of four (4) hours pay at his prevailing rate or given four (4) hours work at the direction of his Foreman, unless he has been notified, or a reasonable attempt has been made to contact the employee by his Foreman or other authorized employee, prior to leaving home, that there will be no work on the day involved.

The four (4) hours will not be paid if an employee declines to accept any work offered him, or if no work can be offered because of conditions beyond the Company's control, such as fire, flood, utility failure, or acts of God.

ARTICLE VII
Seniority

SECTION 1. For the purpose of this Agreement, seniority of the employees subject to this Agreement is defined as the total period of credited employment with the Company from the last day of hire. A new employee retained beyond the probationary period shall be credited with seniority from his date of hire.

SECTION 2. A seniority list of all bargaining unit employees of the Company shall be posted on the bulletin board and revised at least every six (6) months.

SECTION 3. Seniority will be lost by an employee for any of the following reasons:
  (a) If he is discharged for justifiable cause.
  (b) If he voluntarily leaves the service of the Company.
  (c) If he is absent three (3) days without having reported himself off (extenuating circumstances to be considered on an individual basis).
  (d) If an employee has been absent because of layoff or physical disability, he shall continue to be credited for seniority and shall have a right of recall up to a maximum of two (2) years from the date of layoff or onset of physical disability.

SECTION 4. Layoff
  (a) When the workforce is reduced, all probationary employees shall be laid off first. If a further reduction is necessary, layoff will be made starting with the least service on a plant-wide basis provided the remaining employees are qualified to perform the available work and providing that Maintenance employees will be laid off only by lack of work in their respective classification by plant seniority.
  (b) An employee displaced from his job as a result of a layoff will be assigned by the Company to an available job within the Plant. Such assignment will be made in accordance with the preference of such affected employees in seniority order. The affected employees will be required to choose a job in which they have previously performed satisfactorily if such jobs are available. If such a job is not available, the employee will select from the remaining jobs. The employees affected must indicate, by the end of the shift in which the layoff notice is posted, the job they prefer.

SECTION 5. Recall
  (a) Laid off employees will be recalled on the basis of their plant seniority provided they are qualified to perform the available work and provided that Maintenance employees

will be recalled in their respective classification as required by plant seniority.
  (b) A laid-off employee who is recalled to a job other than his bid job will be returned to his bid job when it becomes open. A transferred employee will be returned to his bid job when it becomes open.
  (c) Employees affected by a layoff who refuse to accept recall to a job for which they are qualified will be considered as having quit. Employees affected by a layoff who are not qualified to accept recall to an available job will be continued on layoff without penalty.

ARTICLE VIII
Vacations

SECTION 1. An eligible employee who has attained the years of continuous service indicated in the following table in any calendar year during the continuation of this Agreement, shall receive a vacation corresponding to such years of continuous service as shown in the table:

Years of Service	Vacation
0 - 2	2 weeks
3 - 5	3 weeks
6 - 10	4 weeks
11 - 15	5 weeks
16 - 25	6 weeks
	over 258 weeks

SECTION 2. In order to insure orderly operation in the plants, the Company will schedule vacations to conform to operating requirements, meeting the desires of the employees where practicable. Promptly after January 1st, and before April 1st of each year, each employee eligible for vacation shall be requested to specify in writing the vacation period he desires. Vacation will, insofar as practicable, be granted at times most desired by employees, with longer service employees being given preference as to choice. Vacation commitments will be allowed, once approved, unless the employee agrees to a change. Vacation requests received after April 1st will be given preference after those received during the period January 1st through March 31st. Promptly after April 1st, the Company will prepare and post the vacation schedule of those employees who submitted requests. All eligible employees must

16

request vacation periods by May 1st, at which time the Company will complete the vacation schedule, and applications received thereafter will be scheduled without the right of seniority preference. Vacations desired prior to April 1st may be arranged outside this scheduling procedure.

ARTICLE IX
Adjustment of Grievances

A grievance shall consist of a dispute between an employee, the Union, and the Company as to the meaning or application of any provisions of this Agreement.

When it becomes necessary for a Union officer, steward, or employee to process a grievance during working hours, he shall notify the foreman involved in advance and ring out his card and receive no pay for the time spent processing the grievance. It is the Union's desire that a minimum of time be spent processing the grievances during regular shift hours of the employees and the Union officers concerned.

The President of the Union, or his duly appointed representatives chosen from the Grievance Committee, shall have access to departments other than his own for the purpose of transacting the legitimate business of the grievance procedure, after reasonable notice has been given to the head of the department to be visited and permission from his own department has been obtained.

An employee ordered to report to the office for disciplinary purposes shall have the right to be represented by a Union official (steward, committeeman, or officer). The representative will be treated as though processing a grievance. The employee shall be advised of the purpose of the meeting in advance and advised of the provisions of this paragraph.

The Union Committee or Union officers shall conduct no Union activities, other than processing of grievances, on Company premises without the consent of the Company.

Step 1. Within three (3) working days after the first occurrence of the situation, condition, or actions of the Company giving rise to the grievance, the employee affected shall personally discuss the grievance with his foreman. He shall ring out his card (unless it can be discussed on an off-shift hour) and his steward shall be present.

Within twenty-four (24) hours after the grievance is discussed, the foreman shall give his verbal decision to the aggrieved employee and/or his steward.

Step 2. In the event that a satisfactory settlement has not been reached at the verbal level, the aggrieved employee or his steward may, within 48 hours, present the grievance in writing and within 48 hours shall receive a written answer from his foreman.

Step 3. Within three (3) working days after the written decision has been given, the Local Union may present the grievance in writing to a representative designated by the Company.

All third-step grievances (except discharge cases which may, if requested by the Union, be discussed at special meetings to meet deadlines) shall be considered at the next scheduled grievance meeting attended by an International Representative, unless he waives the right to be present; but upon demand by the Company, such representative shall attend at least one meeting a month to consider pending grievances.

Within four (4) working days after the grievance meeting, the Company shall give the Local Union its written decision. The time limits in this step may be extended by mutual agreement.

The aggrieved, or in case of a group grievance, a representative of the aggrieved group, may be present at the meetings at all steps of this grievance procedure if he so requests to be present.

The Union shall certify in writing to the Company, over the signature of the Local Union Recording Secretary, a list of the officers, committeemen, and stewards who are to be reorganized by the Company.

The Union Grievance Committee shall consist of not less than three (3) members.

The Union Grievance Committee shall have the right to file a grievance on behalf of an employee and/or employees if there is a contract violation, and if filed within three (3) working days of the occurrence.

SUSPENSIONS OR DISCHARGES:
Should the Company determine that an employee should be discharged, he shall first receive a five (5) day suspension, which suspension notice shall be given either orally or in writing, with like notice to the Union. During said five (5) day period, should

such suspended employee feel that he has been unjustly dealt with, he may request and receive a hearing before the Company's Plant Manager, or his representative, in the presence of a Union representative. This shall not apply to probationary employees.

In this event an employee shall be discharged from his employment at the termination of the five (5) day suspension, and if he believes that he has been unjustly dealt with, such discharge shall constitute a grievance to be adjusted under the provisions of the grievance procedure. Such discharged employee shall file his grievance within three (3) working days, and such grievance shall be processed as a third-step grievance.

A special third-step meeting shall be held within four (4) working days, and the Company's answer will be given within three (3) additional working days. The time limit for appeal to arbitration shall be fifteen (15) days from the date of the discharge.

ARBITRATION:

Upon written request and not later than thirty (30) days from the date of the Company's third-step answer, the Union may appeal the grievance to arbitration (except in the case of a suspension or discharge case).

Selection of an arbitrator will be arranged promptly and within ten (10) days. The Company and the Union will select an arbitrator in whom they have mutual confidence. In the event the Company and the Union are unable to agree on an arbitrator, they will apply jointly to the Federal Mediation and Conciliation Service for a panel of five suggested arbitrators. Each party shall alternately cross out two names and the remaining panel member shall be the selected arbitrator.

ARTICLE X
Strikes and Lockouts

SECTION 1. The Union agrees that there shall be no authorized strike, or other drastic action during the life of this Agreement, unless the Company shall refuse to comply with the grievance procedure set forth in this Agreement, or refuse to permit the Union the right to arbitration of any grievance processed through Step 3 of the grievance procedure.

SECTION 2. The Union agrees that if any strike or concerted stoppage of work which is unauthorized or unratified by the Union occurs, the Union will immediately publicly disavow such strike, picketing, slowdown, or stoppage and direct the employees engaged therein to return to work, regardless of the existence of any wildcat picketing. The Company may discipline or discharge any employees continuing to participate therein.

Upon compliance with the foregoing provisions, the Union will not be liable in damages and the Company will not bring suit against the Union in connection with any such unauthorized or unratified strike or stoppage of work.

SECTION 3. The Company agrees that there shall be no lockout during the life of this Agreement unless the Union or its members refuse to comply with the grievance procedure as set forth in this Agreement, or refuse an appeal to arbitration made by the Company.

Reduction in operations determined upon by the Company by reason of lack of sales or reduced volume of sales or conditions beyond the control of the Company shall not be considered as a lockout under this Agreement.

ARTICLE XI
Jury Duty

An employee who is called for jury service or who is subpoenaed as a witness will be excused from work for each such day of service on which he otherwise would have worked, the difference between eight (8) times his average straight time hourly earnings and the payment he receives for such service.

The employee will present proof of service and the amount of pay received therefor.

An employee who notifies the Company at his first opportunity that he has been selected for jury duty will be scheduled to work the day shift, and the Company may make such assignments as necessary among other employees to accomplish the change.

ARTICLE XII
Pay for Injury on The Job

An employee suffering an injury on the job arising out of his work, will receive pay at the rate (either straight time or overtime) he was being paid at the time of the injury for the balance of the shift on which the injury occurred.

18

It shall be the employee's responsibility to obtain the written opinion of the doctor that he is unable to continue to work the balance of the shift and to deliver that opinion to the Company to be eligible for pay for the balance of the day.

ARTICLE XIII
Group Insurance

SECTION 1. The Company shall provide all full-time employees, who have qualified under Article IV, group life insurance, hospitalization, weekly accident and sickness benefits, surgical, maternity, diagnostic x-ray and laboratory fees, and major medical including Dental coverage. A summary description of these agreed to benefits will be made available to covered employees, and the Union shall receive a copy of the Master Policy with the insurance carrier detailing the specifics of the insurance coverage granted. The cost of the above benefits will be paid for by the Company, with the exception of hospitalization and major medical coverage, for which the Company pays one half the cost.

SECTION 2. In the event of a layoff, the Company will pay the benefits provided for the balance of the month during which the layoff occurs. In the event of sick or accident leave, the Company will pay the benefits provided for the balance of the month during which the leave occurs and three (3) additional months. Employees on layoff, sick or accident leave, may continue benefits provided, except for sickness and accident coverage, for five (5) additional months by paying in advance on or before the fifth (5th) day prior to the first (1st) of each month the cost per employee for such coverage to the Company at its office in Sugarcreek. At the end of such period, such employee shall have the privilege of converting such insurance upon complying with such rules and regulations as the insurance company shall require.

SECTION 3. Such program of insurance benefits shall be in substitution for any and all insurance benefits or payments to or on behalf of employees for death, sickness or accident hospitalization, medical or surgical service now provided by the Company in whole or in part (except as benefits under Workmen's Compensation and occupational disease laws) and shall be the exclusive benefit or payment of such nature to be provided in whole or in part by the

Company, except as the Company and the Union shall in writing otherwise expressly agree.

SECTION 4. It is intended that the provisions for insurance benefits which shall be included in such program of insurance benefits shall comply with and be in substitution for provisions for similar benefits which are or shall be made by any law or laws. Amounts required to be paid by the Company, either as contributions, taxes, or benefits under any law or laws providing non-occupational insurance benefits shall reduce to that extent the amount the Company shall likewise be required to pay under this Agreement and appropriate readjustment shall likewise be made in the benefits.

Full co-ordination of benefits will apply to any statutory health plans.

For active employees in areas served by practice plan, qualified under the Health Maintenance Organization Act of 1973, the Company will make arrangements to offer the Union the option to subscribe to such plan in their area instead of group hospitalization, surgical, dental, and/or Major Medical coverage currently provided. The cost to the Company for participating in such qualified group practice plan or in coverage imposed by statute during the life of this Agreement shall not exceed the cost of the current coverage. Any excess of the current cost will be deducted from the pay of each active employee participating in such qualified group practice plan.

ARTICLE XIV
Holiday Pay

SECTION 1. All employees subject to this Agreement, with the exception of probationary employees, without being required to work therefor, shall be paid for each of the following holidays, to-wit: New Year's, Good Friday, Memorial Day, July 4th, Labor Day, Thanksgiving, Christmas, December 24th, the day following Thanksgiving Day, and New Year's Eve.

ARTICLE XV
Production or Direct Work

SECTION 1. The Union recognizes that a high level of productivity is essential for maintaining a secure competitive position. For this reason, the Union and its members will cooperate in attaining a fair day's production from each employee; further, the Union and its members will assist in effecting economies and the utilization of improved methods and equipment.

SECTION 2. Supervisory personnel shall not perform any work normally performed by production employees, except that such supervisory personnel may be required to work in emergencies, in relieving employees for personal time, in instructing employees, in carrying out functions necessary to the fulfillment of their supervisory responsibilities, such as checking workmanship, equipment and maintenance needs, on certain experimental and development projects, and die construction and repair.

ARTICLE XVI
Safety and Working Conditions

SECTION 1. The Union will support the Company in its effort to maintain satisfactory working conditions--especially in regard to safety, good housekeeping and health.

SECTION 2. The Company shall make reasonable provisions for the safety and health of its employees during the hours of their employment. In accordance with practices now prevailing, the Company will furnish, at its own expense, safety glasses, goggles and gloves necessary to safeguard and protect employees from injury. Company furnished items must be returned before replacements will be provided.

SECTION 3. The Company will provide prescription ground safety glasses to those employees whose bid in jobs have been determined to be in areas that are eye hazards; this determination shall be made by the Company and the Union Grievance Committee, based upon the recommendation of the Joint Company and Union Safety Committee. The Company will pay for the glasses and the employee will pay for the prescription.

ARTICLE XVII
Bulletin Boards

Suitable bulletin boards will be provided where proper notices of interest to employees may be posted by the employee's committees, and notices of the Company to employees. Nothing of a controversial or political nature shall be posted.

ARTICLE XVIII
Temporary Assignments

SECTION 1. Temporary working assignments may be made not to exceed 30 calendar days, unless approved by the Union, and such assignments shall not be made on a day-off, day-on basis to circumvent the 30 days provision. Such assignments will be made from the qualified persons first on a voluntary basis, and thereafter the Company will require the least senior qualified person to take the assignment.

After an employee has been assigned to a temporary assignment of five (5) days or less, he will continue on that assignment up to five (5) days; on the sixth day, however, the vacancy will again be offered to the senior qualified person on a voluntary basis. An employee on temporary assignment shall receive his regular rate of pay or the pay of the temporary job, whichever is higher.

SECTION 2. An assignment offered in lieu of work on the employee's regular job due to a curtailment of such work will be paid at the rate of the job taken.

ARTICLE XIX
Leave of Absence

SECTION 1. Whenever the requirements of the plant will permit, and for justifiable cause, any employee shall be granted a leave of absence for a limited time. A record shall be made in duplicate of any leave of absence and a copy given to the Union President. Such leave and any extension thereof shall be by mutual agreement between the Company and the Union.

SECTION 2. Designated members of the Union shall be granted time off, without pay, to perform any Union activities. Notice to the Company shall be given by such designated member of the Union requesting the privilege herein provided for.

SECTION 3. Seniority shall accumulate during such leave of absence, except when the terms of the leave are violated.

SECTION 4. A leave of absence shall be granted to an employee who is elected to a political office.

Such employee shall not accrue continuous service privileges during such leave.

ARTICLE XX
Wages

SECTION 1. Exhibit A on the Personnel office board is a list of job classifications presently worked by employees of the Company, by department and pay grade. A similarly named classification in one department does not necessarily indicate the ability to perform a similarly named classification in another department. Exhibit B attached hereto is a chart of the wage scale of each pay grade, fixing the minimum hiring rate and the top rate of the job. Job classifications named herein are for the purpose of establishing a wage rate and to prescribe the principle function of the job only. The Company and the Union agree that each employee will perform such normal work as has been assigned to the job in the past and shall perform such newly assigned normal and corollary functions as shall be reasonably necessary to the performance of the principle function of the work, such as set ups, clean up, and the handling of materials and tooling. The inclusion of a function in one job shall not exclude the same or similar function from another job.

SECTION 2. New Jobs: When a new job is established or a new machine is acquired, the Company will establish a rate range for the position, as provided in SECTION 1 of this Article, which shall be established as near as reasonably possible on a parity with other like or similar positions existing within the bargaining unit, taking into consideration a comparison of the skill, experience, education, effort and responsibility required of the new position and the comparable positions.

The individuals on the seniority list first placed in the position, or the Union Grievance Committee, may, if it is felt the rate has not been established at a proper level, file a grievance within ten (10) days of commencing the position, which grievance will be adjusted pursuant to the grievance and arbitration sections of the Agreement. There may be only one (1) grievance for each new position, which shall cover the rate range of the position. The decision will be effective from the date the job was established.

SECTION 3. Shift Differential: A shift differential of 10% of base rate pay shall be paid on all hours worked between 4:00 p.m. and 8:00 a.m.

SECTION 4. Clothing Allowance: Each full-time employee with at least 1 year of service shall receive a clothing allowance of $200 on July 1 of each year.

ARTICLE XXI
Overtime

SECTION 1. Weekend overtime will be posted no later than the end of the respective shifts on the Thursday preceding the weekend.

SECTION 2. Daily overtime will be scheduled no later than one (1) hour before the end of the regular shift, or as soon before the end of the shift as the need for the overtime is determined by management.

SECTION 3. Overtime not properly scheduled will be worked on a voluntary basis by eligible employees.

SECTION 4. In case of disagreement as to who shall perform properly scheduled overtime work, it shall be assigned by the Company to the most junior employee in the classification who is fully qualified to immediately perform the work and who must perform the overtime. Overtime not voluntarily accepted shall not be charged against the employee as overtime worked under SECTION 5 hereof.

SECTION 5. Overtime will be divided as equally as is reasonably possible between those persons in the same classification in each department. The Company will maintain a record of chargeable overtime by departments. Overtime worked out of the department or out of classification shall be charged to the person as though worked within his classification and department, subject to the provisions of Section 4.

SECTION 6. All work performed in excess of eight (8) hours in a twenty-four (24) hour day shall be paid for at the rate of time and one-half. Time off but paid for by the Company, including paid vacation time and days during the normal work week when the plant or employee is not scheduled to work, will be treated as time worked for weekly overtime. Time attending scheduled grievance meetings shall be treated as time worked for the purpose of computing weekly overtime.

SECTION 7. <u>Longevity Pay</u>: Employees will receive in their first regular December paycheck longevity pay according to their years of service as of June 1. This amount of pay will be:

Level	Years of Service	Annual Pay
1	6-10	$500
2	11-15	$1,000
3	16-20	$1,500
4	21-25	$2,000
5	26-30	$3,000
6	over 30	$4,000

SECTION 8. The first phase of Section 6 of this Article shall not apply to an early call-in when the employee has had a minimum of ten (10) hours off duty and continues his work following his call-in into his regular shift.

ARTICLE XXII
Part-Time Help

SECTION 1. The Company may, as the need arises from time to time, hire part-time employees. Such part-time employees shall not exercise seniority over any full-time employee in the bargaining unit, nor will they be permitted to participate in any employee benefits.

SECTION 2. Any provision in this Agreement to the contrary notwithstanding the Company may, as the need arises, hire seasonal employees. A seasonal employee is one whose term of employment is not to exceed 120 consecutive days. It is understood and agreed that no seasonal employees will be hired while regular employees are on layoff status. Seasonal employees will be hired and maintained at the then prevailing base rate in the Plant. A seasonal employee shall, as a condition of employment, after the ninetieth (90th) working day from the most recent date of hire, be required to pay the initiation fees and the periodic due to the Union. A seasonal employee shall not, in any other respect, but subject to the terms and conditions of this Agreement.

ARTICLE XXIII
Pensions

Employees with 20 years service are eligible to retire on or after July 1, 1987, shall receive an annual benefit equal to the product of their years of service multiplied by 2% of their highest year's base wage. Base wage is defined as the hourly rate multiplied by 2080. Retired employees shall receive their monthly benefit until death.

ARTICLE XXIV
Term of Agreement

This Agreement shall be effective at 12:01 a.m., June 1, and shall continue in full force and effect until 12:00 a.m., May 31, one year hence. And thereafter it shall be considered to be automatically renewed for successive periods of twelve (12) months, unless more than sixty (60) days prior to the termination of any such twelve (12) month period, either party shall serve written notice upon the other that it desires to cancel, modify or review the Agreement or any provision thereof, or to open it for negotiation of wage rate or economic issues, and in no case shall the Agreement, or any part thereof, be otherwise cancelled, modified, revised, or opened.

EXHIBIT A JOB CLASSIFICATIONS		EXHIBIT B OHIO METALS WAGE SCALE	
GROUP		PAY GROUP	CURRENT HIRE RATE
I	Die Repair	I	$~~12.30~~ 8.36
		II	~~11.95~~ 16.95
II	Maintenance	III	~~11.30~~ 14.36
		IV	~~10.05~~ 14.05
III	Cage Attendant	V	~~9.50~~ 12.56
	Checker A	VI	~~8.95~~ 11.95
	Head Loader	VII	~~8.40~~ 10.40
	Guillotine Operator	VIII	~~7.90~~ 9.90
	Brake Operator		
	Crane Operator		
	Automatic Door Bander		
IV	K. D. Material Handling		
	Utility		
	Checker B		
	Glass Cutter (Big Glass)		
	Punch Press Operator (Large)		
	Loading		
	Receiving		
	Plant Truck Driver		
V	Salvage		
	Material Handling		
	Janitor		
	Schlegel		
VII	Inspection		
	Sample Building		
	Casement Building		
	Glass Cutting		
	Parts Puller (Sash, Frame, and Screen)		
VII	Saw Operator		
	Belt Line		
	Door Prehanging		
	Screen Pre-Assembly		
	Screening		
VIII	Sash Building		
	Window Frame Builder		
	Factory Clerical		

KEY ECONOMIC FEATURES OF CURRENT AGREEMENT

WAGES

Wage Group	Effective Rate, (Column A) June 1	No. Employees (Column B) in Group
I	$12.30 *18.30*	45
II	11.95 *16.95*	63
III	11.30 *14.30*	56
IV	10.05 *14.05*	143
V	9.50 *12.50*	210
VI	8.95 *11.95*	82
VII	8.40 *10.40*	62
VIII	7.90 *9.90*	37
		698

Wage Cost per hour
in each wage group
(Column A times B)

$ 553.50	*823.50*
752.85	*1,067.85*
632.80	*800.80*
1,437.15	*2,009.15*
1,995.00	*2,625.00*
733.90	*979.90*
520.80	*644.80*
292.30	*366.30*
$6,918.30	*9,317.30*

Average Hourly Rate per employee = $6,918.30 *9,317.30* / 698 employees = $9.9116 *13.3486*

Payroll cost per year = $6,918.30 *9,317.30*/hr. x 52 weeks. x 40 hrs. per wk.= $14,390,064 *19,379,984.00*
excludes roll-up (e.g. fringe costs - see next page)

25

ROLL-UP   Cost increases directly attributable to wages paid including: social security (employer's share); life insurance premiums; overtime premium; pension benefits. If any individual roll-up item is increased during negotiations, then the roll-up percentage must also be increased. The programmed percentage does not change. The following table depicts these items:

Benefit	% Increase
Social Security	7.51
Group Insurance Premium	.12
Overtime Premium (based on past experiences of 8 hours per week = Avg. overtime per year)	3.40
Pension Benefit	6.87
	17.90%

Total Annual Payroll Cost = Payroll (~~$14,390,064~~) + Roll Up (~~$14,390,064~~ x .179) =
~~$16,965,885~~   19,379,984   19,379,984
22,849,001

PAID TIME OFF

Holidays: 10 paid holidays per year in current contract

Total Cost per year = 698 employees x 10 days x 8 hrs./day x ~~9.9116 avg.~~ 13.3486 hourly rate =
~~$553,463.74~~
745,385.82

CLOTHING ALLOWANCE

Current contract: ~~$200~~ 300. per year for each employee with at least 1 yr. of service.

Total Cost per year: ~~$200.00~~ 300 x 670 = ~~$134,000.~~
261,000

only 670 with more than 1 yr total
Still 698 employees all together

26

VACATION DAYS

Vacation Schedule (As of June 1)

Service	A Vacation	B No. Employees	C Average Hourly Rate per Employee	D Cost per Day	A×B×D E Avg cost per yr
0 - 2 years	2 weeks *10 days*	220	~~$ 8.30~~ *10.36*	~~$66.40~~ *82.40*	*181,286*
3 - 5 years	3 weeks *15 days*	143	~~9.55~~ *11.55*	~~76.40~~ *92.40*	*198,198*
6 - 10 years	4 weeks *20 days*	183	~~10.85~~ *12.85*	~~86.80~~ *102.80*	*376,248*
11 - 15 years	5 weeks *25 days*	87	~~11.05~~ *14.05*	~~88.40~~ *112.40*	*244,470*
16 - 25 years	6 weeks *30 days*	57	~~11.50~~ *15.50*	~~92.00~~ *124.00*	*212,040*
over 25 years	8 weeks *40 days*	8	~~12.10~~ *18.30*	~~96.80~~ *146.40*	*46,848*
		698			*1,259,084*

The Current Annual Cost of Vacations is ~~$1,008,212.00~~
1,259,084.00

HEALTH INSURANCE (Hospitalization and Major Medical)

Type of Coverage	Annual Premium	Number of Employees	
Single	*1,440.00* ~~$980~~	275	*113/week = Now (bi)*
Family	*3,660.00* ~~$2,520~~	335	*175/week = Sta (bi)*
		610	*max = 90/biweekly*

Current Annual Cost to Employer* = 610 x ~~$490~~ *720* = ~~$298,900~~
439,200

* 88 employees have not signed up for health insurance, possibly due to coverage by a spouse's employer. Current contract provides that employer pays one half of the single coverage premium only (e.g., ~~$490 of $980).~~
(720 of 1440)

For family coverage, employee pays 2,940 (3,660 - 720)

27

LONGEVITY PAY

Current Schedule:

Level		Annual Pay	No. Employees As of June 1	Total Annual Cost
1	6 yrs. - 10 yrs. Service	$500.	183	$ 91,500.
2	11 yrs. - 15 yrs. Service	$1,000. ~~750~~	87	$ 87,000.
3	16 yrs. - 20 yrs. Service	$1,500. 1000	35	$ 52,500.
4	21 yrs. - 25 yrs. Service	$2,000. 1500	22	$ 44,000.
5	26 yrs. - 30 yrs. Service	$3,000. 2000	~~5~~ 3	$~~15,000.~~ 9,000
~~6~~	~~over 30 yrs. Service~~	~~$4,000.~~	~~3~~	~~$ 12,000.~~
				~~$302,000.~~
				284,000

SHIFT DIFFERENTIAL

Current contract: 10% shift differential for all hours worked on a shift regularly scheduled between 4:00 pm. and 8:00 am.

Wage Group	Rate	x 10%	x Eligible Employees. On Shift	= Hourly Cost
I	12.30	1.23	18	22.14
II	11.95	1.20	46	55.20
III	11.30	1.13	43	48.59
IV	10.05	1.01	70	70.70
V	9.50	.95	103	97.85
VI	8.95	.90	38	34.20
VII	8.40	.84	30	25.20
VIII	7.90	.79	17	13.43
			365	367.31

Annual Cost of Shift Differential = $367.31 per hour x 40 hours per week x 52 weeks = $764,004

PLAYER'S ROLES

Negotiating teams may find it useful to assign specific roles to each member to provide the variety of expertise and backgrounds commonly found at a negotiating table. The role descriptions on the following pages will help each team member determine how to prepare to take part in their team's negotiations and can balance the workload among all team members. Participants are not limited to the duties and responsibilities suggested, in fact, they are encouraged to expand the role according to the overall strategy developed with their team members. If a team has fewer than five members, the duties of those players' roles left unfilled should be added to their players.

Management   Union

Chief Negotiator   President, Local 56
Human Resource Manager   Vice President, Local 56
Production Manager   Business Agent
Quality Control Supervisor   Shop Steward
Chief Supervisor   Chair, Grievance Committee

Chief Negotiator

You are the labor attorney hired by the company president to lead the management team. Since you only work with the rest of the management team during the negotiating process you must build a consensus of the team on each bargaining issue and proposal. President Barry has made it clear to you, however, that the team must accurately forecast what level of total personnel costs the company pays and then only agree to a total economic package which is within that figure.

During negotiations you should insist that the other team members allow only you to make or accept "formal" proposals on issues while "informal" proposals can be discussed by any team member. This could be provided in negotiation ground rules adopted by both teams.

It is primarily your responsibility to develop an overall negotiation strategy for management. For example, before negotiations begin you should decide, with your team members, whether you plan to "package" items for proposals and counter-proposals, or negotiate only one item at a time; decide which high priority items management must achieve in the final agreement; and make sure the final economic package is one which management will be able to pay in the future.

Overall, you want to avoid a strike, if possible, while only agreeing to a contract which will keep Ohio Metals profitable.

Human Resource Manager

You provide vital information to the chief negotiator and the other management team members. As the HRM (personnel) specialist you are the only team member who understands the details of the economic items in the current agreement. You should take the lead in preparing the economic priorities for management. Therefore you are the "numbers" person who must determine the cost of each item in each proposal. In addition, you will provide the estimated cost of the final agreement. You have prepared yourself for this role by learning the "costing" portion of the student computer disk. Thus, you can easily access the program on the disk to cost out most of the economic proposals made by either side during negotiations. The few which cannot be directly made by the costing program on the disk can probably be made with only one or two simple mathematical calculations using the disk information or the pages in this manual which contain the key economic features of the current agreement.

One of your team members may keep a log book of the negotiations. Your responsibilities include maintaining a "costing" section in the log book which will include a copy of each proposal you cost out for the team, including the cost estimates of each of the proposals made by the labor team. The first page of the costing section should be an index of the material which follows. This information is essential to your teammates who must use it to assess the value or cost of each proposal before it is offered by the management team, or before a labor team proposal is accepted. You should keep a copy of the items your have costed out. (You could use the "print screen" feature on your computer to print the pages from the computer program.) Overall your job is to provide your team with cost estimates of proposals from both sides so the team can accurately evaluate them.

Production Manager

You have two primary roles on the management team. The first is to use your years of experience in production at Ohio Metals to evaluate the non-economic items and proposals which arise during negotiations. You should take the lead in developing the non-economic priorities of the management team. In addition, you should anticipate and prepare to respond to the non-economic proposals made by the labor team.

The second role centers on your extended knowledge of the current agreement. Since you have been involved in the adjustment of grievances for many years, you are relied upon as the most knowledgeable team member in matters concerning the content of the agreement. Thus, you should carefully review the current agreement to determine what "language" changes should be proposed by management to clarify vague or incomplete sections.

You should also write the final version of the new agreement containing all of the negotiated changes.

Quality Control Supervisor

You have been assigned the role of developing and maintaining a record of all aspects of the management team's preparation and participation in this contract negotiation. The skills in organization and attention to detail which you have displayed as quality control supervisor caused the president to assign you this role. This record is important to management because it is the only permanent source of the minutes of negotiation sessions, formal proposals and counter-proposals, industry information, costing data, etc. Thus you, as in past negotiations, prepare a three-ring binder with all the team's information organized by section. The most important section of this "log" book is your written minutes of <u>each</u> team meeting from the very first session.

It is very important that you delineate in the minutes the strategy decisions made by the management team. This discussion should include why items are given high or low priorities, and the reasons for offering each proposal as well as those for accepting or rejecting the proposals of the labor team. The Human Resource Manager should provide the costing information for the log, and the Production Manager should provide the analysis of all non-economic items and proposals.

Another important role for your position is to analyze the strategy and proposals made by both sides. You should alert your teammates during caucuses or negotiations if they are deviating from the overall management strategy. It may be helpful to date and consecutively number each proposal/counter-proposal made by each side (M1, M2, M3; L1, L2, L3, etc.) to provide a chronology of the negotiations.

Chief Supervisor

Every negotiating team needs one member to continually plead its case. This is your role on the management team. Some would call you the "agitator" who constantly complains that union members are overpaid and looking for ways to make their jobs easier. As a former union worker and union negotiator at Ohio Metals you know the history of both sides, and you know "the tricks." Thus, your team expects you to be loud and irritating to labor during negotiating sessions. At the same time you constantly remind the union of what nonunion workers are receiving and how competitive the industry has become in recent years.

Another part of your role is to perform library research to substantiate management's position on economic and non-economic issues. This information can be both a basis for management's decisions and a source of support to present to the labor team.

President, Local 56

You are the local union president, elected by your union members to represent them in matters of labor relations. You realize that as chief negotiator of the union's negotiating team you must represent the interests of all the union members to the best of your ability. The role of chief negotiator is by far the most important duty of the president's job. The survey of employee preferences you have conducted gives you a clear idea of which negotiating items are most important to your members.

From past experience, however, it is clear that the members do not expect you to win all of their top demands. They also expect that you will not walk away empty handed. In recent years you have convinced them to be patient, and they were. But the company has recovered substantially, in their minds, and they want to share in the "good times as well as the bad."

During negotiations you should insist that the other team members allow only you to make or accept "formal" proposals while "informal" proposals can be made by any team member. This could be provided in the negotiated ground rules.

Your most important responsibility is the development of an overall negotiation strategy for the union team. Before negotiations begin, for example, together with the rest of your team you should decide which high priority economic and non-economic items the union must achieve in the final agreement; should the union propose to negotiate one item at a time, a "package" of several items, or should the entire agreement be put on the table for discussion at the same time. You should also discuss whether the union's strategy will be to take the offensive during negotiations, or wait to respond to management proposals.

Overall, you want to avoid a strike which would be very costly to your members, however you realize that significant gains must be achieved for them to vote to ratify any proposed agreement.

Chair, Grievance Committee

Every negotiating team needs one member to continually plead its case. This is your role on the union team. Some would call you the "agitator" who constantly complains that management is abusing workers and blaming the union for problems caused by management. As a union worker and former union vice president you know the history of both sides, and you know "the tricks." Thus, your team expects you to be a source of irritation to management during negotiating sessions. At the same time you constantly remind management of the pay and benefits workers are receiving and how competitive the industry has become in recent years.

Another part of your role is to perform library research to substantiate the union's position on economic and non-economic issues. This information can be both a basis for the union's decisions and a source of support to present to the management team.

Vice-President, Local 56

Your role is to provide most of the vital detailed information to the union president and chief negotiator. You are the only team member with the background and experience to understand the details of the economic items in the current agreement. Your role, therefore, is to take the lead in preparing the economic priorities and proposals for the union. As the "numbers" person for the union your job also includes costing out the economic proposals made by management. In addition, you will determine the estimated cost of the final agreement.

In preparation for this role you have learned the "costing" portion of the computer disk. Therefore, you should be able to easily access the program on the disk and cost out the economic proposals made by either side during negotiations. If any cannot be directly made from the costing program you should be able to develop cost estimates with simple mathematical calculations using the disk information or the pages in this manual which contain the key economic features of the agreement.

Your responsibilities also include providing the "costing" section of the team's log book, which will be kept by one of your teammates. The costing section should include a copy of each proposal you cost out for the team, including the cost estimates of management's economic proposals. The first page of the costing section should be an index of the material which follows. This information is critical to your teammates who must use it to assess the value or worth of each proposal before it is given to management, or before one of management's economic proposals is accepted. You should keep a copy of the items you have costed out.

Overall, your job is to provide your teammates with cost estimates of all proposals in order that they can effectively evaluate them.

Business Agent

You have two primary roles on the union team. The first is to utilize your many years of experience in the union to provide an evaluation of the non-economic items and proposals which arise during negotiations. You should take the lead in developing the non-economic items and proposals which arise during negotiations. You should take the lead in developing the non-economic priorities of the union team. In addition, you should anticipate and be prepared to respond to the non-economic proposals made by management.

The second role you assume in negotiations centers on your extended knowledge of the current agreement. Since you have been involved in the adjustment of grievances for several years, you are relied upon as the most knowledgeable team member in matters concerning the content of the agreement. Thus you should carefully review the current agreement to determine what "language" changes should be proposed by management to clarify vague or incomplete sections. You should also write the final version of the new agreement containing all of the negotiated changes.

Shop Steward

Your primary role on the union negotiation team is to develop and maintain a written record of all aspects of the team's preparation and participation in this round of negotiations. This record, or "log," is an important part of the negotiation effort because it is the only permanent source of minutes (of the strategy and negotiation sessions), formal proposals, counter-proposals, industry information, costing data, etc. As you have done in the past, you should prepare a three-ring binder with all the team's information organized by section. The most important section of the log book is your written minutes of <u>each</u> team meeting from your very first session including all caucuses, planning and negotiation sessions. You should delineate in the minutes the overall strategy developed by the union, why items are given high or low priority, the reasons for offering proposals, and a rationale for accepting or rejecting the proposals of the management team. The Vice President should provide the costing information for the log, and the Business Agent should provide the analysis of all non-economic items and proposals.

Another important role for your position is to analyze the strategy and proposals made by both sides. During team caucuses you should warn the team if their decisions are not in agreement with the overall strategy and priorities. It may be helpful to date and consecutively number each proposal/counter-proposal made by each side (L1, L2, L3; M1, M2, M3, etc.) to provide a chronology of the negotiations.

SIMULATION FORMS

For Non-Computerized Negotiations

Form A	Calculation of Profits Available Under the New Contract	May be completed at any time
Form B	Initial Non-Economic Priorities	To be completed prior to first session
Form C	Initial Economic Priorities	To be completed prior to first session
Form D	Ground Rules	To be negotiated during first session
Form E	Initial Demands	To be presented immediately after negotiation of ground rules
Form F	Proposal/Counter-proposal	To be completed when official additional proposals and counter-proposals are needed
Form G	Final Agreement	To be signed and dated by labor and management officials
Form H	Estimated Cost of Final Agreement	To be completed by each team after Form F is signed
Form I	Audit of Negotiation	To be completed by audit team
Form J	Appraisal of Individual Performance	To be completed on the last day
Form K	Simulation Evaluation	To be completed on the last day

Form A

CALCULATION OF PROFITS AVAILABLE UNDER THE NEW CONTRACT

This form may be used by both management and labor to calculate the dollar amount each believes to be available for the new contract. Of course, each side may make different assumptions about the firm's future sales, profits, and productivity.

		Current	Projected
1.	Sales (See page 5)	$47,324,000	_____
2.	Production Costs	-23,100,000	_____
3.	Labor Costs (Wages and Benefits)	-16,965,000	_____
4.	Administration and Selling Costs	-2,800,000	_____
5.	Overhead	-1,550,000	_____
6.	Net Profit before Taxes	4,909,000	_____
7.	Income Tax	-2,020,000	_____
8.	Profit After Tax	2,889,000	_____
9.	Dividends Paid	- 400,000	_____
10.	Net Profit	2,489,000	_____

Form B
Reference Use Only

INITIAL NON-ECONOMIC PRIORITIES

Item	Current Provision (cite article #)	Desired Provision	Highest (Mgmt.) or Lowest (Union) Acceptable Provision	Rationale and Priority Weight (total = 100%)

Form C
Reference Use Only

INITIAL ECONOMIC PRIORITIES

Item	Current Provision (cite article #)	Desired Provision	Highest (Mgmt.) or Lowest (Union) Acceptable Provision	Desired Provision Estimated Cost (During 1st Year of Contract)	Rationale and Priority Weight (total=100%)

Form D

GROUND RULES

Proposed by Management   Proposed by Union   Agreed Upon Ground Rules

Union_____ Date_____
Mgmt_____Date_____

43

Form E

INITIAL DEMANDS

Date offered: _____
By team: _____

<u>Name of Item</u>   <u>Demand</u>

Form F

PROPOSAL/COUNTER-PROPOSAL

Date offered: _____

By team: _____

<u>Name of Item</u>   <u>Demand</u>

Form F

PROPOSAL/COUNTER-PROPOSAL

Date offered: _____

By team: _____

<u>Name of Item</u>   <u>Demand</u>

Form F

PROPOSAL/COUNTER-PROPOSAL

Date offered: _____

By team: _____

<u>Name of Item</u>   <u>Demand</u>

Form G

FINAL AGREEMENT

Union: _____ Date: _____

Mgmt: _____ Date: _____

Name of Item	Article #	Contract Clause (Underline Changed or Added Language)

Form H

ESTIMATED COST OF FINAL AGREEMENT

Team: _____
Date: _____

Name of Item	Article #	Calculation of Estimated Annual Cost (Label "Non-Economic" if Appropriate)

TOTAL COST OF FINAL AGREEMENT $ _____

Form I

AUDIT OF NEGOTIATION PERFORMANCE

Team # _____

Audit of Team # _____

Check the appropriate rating of the team's performance during negotiations:

	Poor	Below Average	Average	Above Average	Outstanding
1. Preparation of Non-Economic Priorities (Form B)	___	___	___	___	___
2. Preparation of Economic Priorities (Form C)	___	___	___	___	___
3. Negotiated Ground Rules (Form D)	___	___	___	___	___
4. Initial Demands and Counterproposals (Forms E and F)	___	___	___	___	___
5. Clarity of Final Agreement	___	___	___	___	___
6. Content of Final Agreement (Form G)	___	___	___	___	___
7. Accuracy of Estimated Costs (Form H)	___	___	___	___	___
8. Negotiation Strategy	___	___	___	___	___
9. Balance of Economic and Non-Economic Items	___	___	___	___	___
10. Professionalism of Performance	___	___	___	___	___

Form J

APPRAISAL OF INDIVIDUAL PERFORMANCE

Name _____

Team _____

The purpose of this form is for each person to evaluate the contribution made by each individual team member during the negotiation simulation. Personnel appraisal is one of the responsibilities of every manager; you may not want nor like to rate another person, but you may as well get some practice now. All members should be evaluated on their <u>total</u> performance during the <u>entire</u> process. Appraise each person (including yourself) using the following scale:

5 = Outstanding
4 = Above Average
3 = Average
2 = Below Average
1 = Poor

<u>Name</u>	Atten- dance and Parti- <u>cipation</u>	Contri- bution of Ideas & <u>Strategy</u>	Ability To Negotiate With Other <u>Team</u>	Knowledge of Collective <u>Bargaining</u>	Prepara- tion of <u>Information</u>
1. _____	_____	_____	_____	_____	_____
2. _____	_____	_____	_____	_____	_____
3. _____	_____	_____	_____	_____	_____
4. _____	_____	_____	_____	_____	_____
5. _____	_____	_____	_____	_____	_____

Form K

SIMULATION EVALUATION

Name _____

Class _____

Company # _____

Summarize what you have gained from this Collective Bargaining Exercise:

INTRODUCTION TO THE COMPUTER PROGRAMS

There are two parts to this computerized simulation format. The first program, titled COST, allows you to experiment with different aspects of the contract to determine the cost of each alternative change that may be proposed during negotiations.

The second part (NEGOTIATION) simulates the collective bargaining process between a firm and its union. The union contract reproduced in its entirety in this package is used as the basis for this program. Thus, you should familiarize yourself with the scenario provided in the opening pages of the booklet as well as the contract itself.

You are management, the computer will negotiate for labor. The current contract will expire in four weeks and you have time for about eight bargaining sessions before the expiration date. The union has been very militant in its attitude up to this point and the workers feel they have some "catching up" to do in terms of financial and nonfinancial aspects of the contract. The union has a rather sizable strike fund that it can use for the welfare of its workers, while the firm has about 4-5 weeks of finished goods in inventory. IF NEGOTIATIONS DO NOT PROCEED IN A GOOD FAITH MANNER, THE UNION WILL LIKELY STRIKE. In this case, you would have about 4-5 weeks of inventory to sell then your firm would suffer a great financial loss and possibly go out of business.

You should run the COST program first to learn the cost increases associated with each of the contract provisions. It is critical that management be able to pay any negotiated change in the contract. The program is self-explanatory and you can easily follow the instructions as you proceed through the simulation.

On the next page is the listing of the union's initial economic and non-economic demands. The following pages contain samples of the actual negotiation program and forms which will be completed by you during negotiations.

INITIAL UNION NON-ECONOMIC DEMANDS for computerized negotiations

1 - All bargaining unit jobs posted and filled through seniority only.

2 - Overtime assigned by seniority within job classification on a voluntary basis only.

3 - Drug testing only for probable cause.

4 - Part-time employees could be hired only with the approval of the union.

5 - No subcontracting of work already performed in the unit without union approval.

6 - Union to select cafeteria operator.

7 - One year contract.

(There are four possible alternatives which can be negotiated for each of these non-economic items.)

The union has also presented the following economic demands for meeting the first meeting. All figures shown are for one year and are net additions to current contract provisions.

UNION ECONOMIC DEMANDS

Wages - %	8
Holidays - New Days	2
Funeral Leave - Days	3
Health Ins - Cost	$ 870
Clothing - Cost (per year)	$ 50
Pension - Benefit (per mo.)	$ 100
Vacation - New Days	2
Longevity - Cost (total per yr.)	$30,200
Shift Pay - Additional %	2
Profit-sharing (% of net profit)	33

Note: The firm's financial condition is shown on page 5.

SIMULATION FORMS

For Computerized Negotiations

Form L	Initial Non-Economic Priorities	To be completed prior to first computer session
Form M	Initial Economic Priorities	To be completed prior to first computer session
Form N	Initial Counter-proposal	To be presented prior to first computer session
Form O	Additional Counter-proposal	To be prepared prior to each additional computer negotiation session
Form P	Simulation Evaluation	To be completed on the last day

INITIAL NON-ECONOMIC PRIORITIES

Item	Current Provision (cite article #)	Desired Provision	Highest (Mgmt) or Lowest (Union) Acceptable Provision	Rationale and Priority Weight (total=100%)

INITIAL ECONOMIC PRIORITIES

Item	Current Provision (cite article #)	Desired Provision	Highest (Mgmt) or Lowest Acceptable Provision	Desired Provision Estimated Cost (During 1st Year of Contract)	Rationale and Priority Weight (total=100%)

Form N   **INITIAL COMPANY COUNTER-PROPOSAL**

Session No. _____   Company No. _____

Non-Economic Issues	Union Proposal	Company Offer
1. Job Posting		
2. Overtime Policy		
3. Drug Testing Policy		
4. Part-time Employment Policy		
5. Subcontracting Policy		
6. Cafeteria Policy		
7. Length of Contract		

Economic Issues		
1. Wages (% increase)	_____	_____
2. Paid Holidays-no. of addl. days	_____	_____
3. Funeral Leave -no. of days	_____	_____
4. Health Ins. Cost paid by Company	_____	_____
5. Clothing Allowance	_____	_____
6. Pension Benefits (Additional monthly benefit)	_____	_____
7. Vacation (additional days)	_____	_____
8. Longevity Pay (Additional total cost)	_____	_____
9. Shift Differential (%)	_____	_____
10. Profit Sharing (% of profits)	_____	_____
Total Package Cost	$ _____	$ _____

Form O   **COMPANY COUNTER-PROPOSAL**

Session No. _____   Company No. _____

Non-Economic Issues	Union Proposal	Company Offer
1. Job Posting		
2. Overtime Policy		
3. Drug Testing Policy		
4. Part-time Employment Policy		
5. Subcontracting Policy		
6. Cafeteria Policy		
7. Length of Contract		

Economic Issues

	Union Proposal	Company Offer
1. Wages (% increase)	_____	_____
2. Paid Holidays-no. of addl. days	_____	_____
3. Funeral Leave -no. of days	_____	_____
4. Health Ins. Cost paid by Company	_____	_____
5. Clothing Allowance	_____	_____
6. Pension Benefits (Additional monthly benefit)	_____	_____
7. Vacation (additional days)	_____	_____
8. Longevity Pay (Additional total cost)	_____	_____
9. Shift Differential (%)	_____	_____
10. Profit Sharing (% of profits)	_____	_____
Total Package Cost	$ _____	$ _____

Form P   **SIMULATION EVALUATION**

Name _____

Class _____

Company # _____

Summarize what you have gained from this Collective Bargaining exercise:

NEGOTIATION

ROUTINE

For Collective Bargaining Simulation

Written By
Jerald Smith
Michael Carrell
Peggy Golden

COPYRIGHT 1996   PRENTICE HALL   VERSION 4.0

IS THIS A CONTINUATION OF PREVIOUS NEGOTIATIONS (C)
OR THE START OF A NEW GAME (N)?

ENTER C OR N AND PRESS ENTER: N

INPUT THE 6 DIGIT I.D. NUMBER FROM YOUR INSTRUCTOR
& PRESS ENTER. IF NONE, INPUT A ZERO & PRESS ENTER: 100231

THIS SIMULATION ALLOWS YOU TO NEGOTIATE A CONTRACT WITH
THE UNION WHICH REPRESENTS THE HOURLY WORKERS IN YOUR
FIRM.

THE CONTRACT WILL EXPIRE IN FOUR WEEKS.

THE UNION HAS BEEN VERY MILITANT IN ITS ATTITUDE UP TO
THIS POINT AND THE WORKERS FEEL THEY HAVE SOME CATCHING
UP TO DO BOTH IN THE FINANCIAL AND NON-FINANCIAL AREAS.

THE UNION HAS A RATHER SIZABLE STRIKE FUND THAT
IT CAN USE FOR THE WELFARE OF ITS WORKERS.

YOU WILL HAVE TIME FOR ABOUT 8 NEGOTIATING SESSIONS
BEFORE THE EXPIRATION OF THE CONTRACT.

The information below is the scenario you will be working with in the computer negotiating program:

```
*** CURRENT INFORMATION ***

PRODUCTIVITY INCREASE
SINCE LAST CONTRACT                         5%

INVENTORY LEVEL (STATED
IN WEEKS OF SALES)                           5

LAST YEAR'S PROFITS              $3,064,000

PROFIT/WORKER RATIO                 $4,389

UNION'S STRIKING FUND             $350,000

INDUSTRY AVERAGE WAGE INCREASE:     2.0%
IND. AVG. PRODUCTIVITY INCREASE     2.9%

LOCAL UNEMPLOYMENT                  6.9%
COST OF LIVING LAST YR              2.0%
             TO CONTINUE, PRESS ENTER KEY:
```

```
THE CURRENT SITUATION FOLLOWS:

THE UNION HAS PRESENTED THE FOLLOWING DEMANDS
FOR MEETING 1.  ALL FIGURES SHOWN ARE NET ADDITIONS.

    WAGES - %                              8.00
    HOLIDAYS - # NEW DAYS                     2
    FUNERAL LEAVE - DAYS                      3
    HEALTH INS - COST                      870
    CLOTHING - COST (per Yr)                50
    PROFIT SHARING (% OF NET PROF)          33
    PENSION - BENEFIT (per month)          100
    VACATION - NEW DAYS                      2
    LONGEVITY - Total Cost per Yr $      30,200
    SHIFT PAY - ADDITIONAL %                 2
             TO CONTINUE, PRESS ENTER KEY:
```

THE UNION IS ALSO DEMANDING THESE (NON-FINANCIAL)
CONTRACT PROVISIONS:

*** UNION NON-ECONOMIC DEMANDS ***

1 - All bargaining unit jobs posted and filled through seniority only.

2 - Overtime assigned by seniority within job classification on a voluntary basis only.

3 - Drug testing only for probable cause.

4 - Part-time employees could be hired only with the approval of the union.

5 - No subcontracting of work already performed in the unit without union approval.

6 - Union to select cafeteria operator.

7 - One year contract.

TO CONTINUE, PRESS ENTER KEY:

YOU MUST NOW MAKE A COUNTER OFFER TO THE UNION.

YOU SHOULD HAVE ALREADY USED THE 'COST' PROGRAM TO
ASCERTAIN WHAT YOUR OFFER IS GOING TO COST.

IF YOU HAVE NOT USED THIS PROGRAM YET, YOU MAY TRANSFER TO
IT USING THE MENU WHICH FOLLOWS.

TO CONTINUE, PRESS ENTER KEY:

NOTE: For each of the contract provisions shown above there are four possible alternatives
you may select. These are listed later in the program.

```
**  PROGRAM SELECTION  **

1. CONTINUE THIS NEGOTIATION PROGRAM

2. TRANSFER TO THE COSTING PROGRAM

3. REVIEW THE CURRENT SITUATION

4. REVIEW THE UNION'S DEMANDS

5. PRINT A COPY OF THE CURRENT SITUATION & DEMANDS

6. EXIT THIS PROGRAM

ENTER YOUR CHOICE (1,2,3,4,5,6) AND PRESS ENTER:  1
```

IN ORDER TO AID IN THE NEGOTIATIONS, THE PROGRAM IS DIVIDED INTO TWO PARTS. THE FIRST PART ALLOWS YOU TO INPUT THE NON-ECONOMIC ELEMENTS OF YOUR OFFER AND THE SECOND PART CONTAINS THE FINANCIAL ELEMENTS.

NOTE: If you have costed out the various possibilities, you would continue the program. Otherwise you may want to transfer to the COSTING program to try various combinations of offers.

TO CONTINUE, PRESS ENTER KEY:

SECTION I: THIS PART OF THE PROGRAM ALLOWS YOU TO MAKE AN OFFER OR COUNTER OFFER TO THE UNION ON THE NON-ECONOMIC ISSUES. THE FOLLOWING MENU LISTS THESE ISSUES:

** NON-ECONOMIC ISSUES MENU **
1 - Job Posting Program
2 - Overtime Policy
3 - Drug Testing Policy
4 - Part-time employment
5 - Subcontracting Policy
6 - Cafeteria Management
7 - Length of Contract
8 - Non Economic Issues Complete; go to next step
9 - Restart program from the beginning
10 - Review your non-economic offer

INPUT YOUR CHOICE & PRESS ENTER KEY: 6

In this case item #6, Cafeteria Food, was selected. The various alternatives for this are shown below.

CHOOSE YOUR RESPONSE IN REGARD TO CAFETERIA FOOD:

1 - Union to select cafeteria operator
2 - Union and Management to jointly select cafeteria operator
3 - Union to have representation of the cafeteria committee
4 - Company to control cafeteria as it is now doing

INPUT YOUR CHOICE & PRESS ENTER KEY: 2

After you have selected a response to a non-economic issue, the program will revert to the menu again:

SECTION I: THIS PART OF THE PROGRAM ALLOWS YOU TO MAKE AN OFFER OR COUNTER OFFER TO THE UNION ON THE NON-ECONOMIC ISSUES. THE FOLLOWING MENU LISTS THESE ISSUES:

** NON-ECONOMIC ISSUES MENU **

1 - Job Posting Program
2 - Overtime Policy
3 - Drug Testing Policy
4 - Part-time employment
5 - Subcontracting Policy
 * 6 - Cafeteria Management
7 - Length of Contract
8 - Non Economic Issues Complete; go to next step
9 - Restart program from the beginning
10 - Review your non-economic offer

INPUT YOUR CHOICE & PRESS ENTER KEY: 8

NOTE: An asterisk (*) will placed beside each item that you have made an offer on so you can keep track of your offers.

You may continue to deal with the non-economic issues or, as in the example above, transfer to the economic issues. The response above will transfer the program to the economic section.

SECTION II: THIS PART OF THE PROGRAM ALLOWS YOU TO MAKE A
COUNTER OFFER ON THE FINANCIAL ISSUES OF THE CONTRACT. THE
FOLLOWING MENU LISTS THESE ISSUES:

    TO CONTINUE, PRESS ENTER KEY:

```
*** CONTRACT PROVISION MENU ***

1 - WAGES FOR 8 WAGE GROUPS
2 - PAID HOLIDAYS
3 - FUNERAL LEAVE
4 - HEALTH INSURANCE COST
5 - CLOTHING ALLOWANCE
6 - PROFIT SHARING
7 - PENSION BENEFITS
8 - VACATION
9 - LONGEVITY PLAN
10 - SHIFT DIFFERENTIAL

11 - ALL ISSUES FOR THIS OFFER HAVE BEEN ENTERED
12 - RESTART PROGRAM AT FINANCIAL ISSUES
13 - RESTART PROGRAM AT THE VERY BEGINNING
14 - REVIEW THE CURRENT UNION DEMANDS

INPUT YOUR CHOICE AND PRESS ENTER:  1
```

Note: These 10 items are the economic (financial) issues presented by the union. You may
deal with one at a time and when finished the menu will scroll up again for your next
selection. Wage levels was selected in the example above. The current rates are printed out
as shown below:

```
CURRENT WAGE LEVELS ARE AS FOLLOWS:

GROUP 1 -      12.30
GROUP 2 -      11.95
GROUP 3 -      11.30
GROUP 4 -      10.05
GROUP 5 -       9.50
GROUP 6 -       8.95
GROUP 7 -       8.40
GROUP 8 -       7.90

DO YOU WANT TO APPLY A CONSTANT % INCREASE TO ALL WAGE LEVELS
(P) OR SPECIFY A WAGE FOR EACH GROUP (E)?

INPUT P OR E AND PRESS ENTER:  P
```

```
WHAT PERCENT INCREASE DO YOU WANT TO APPLY TO ALL GROUPS
(INPUT AS A WHOLE NUMBER)?  4
                                    Per Hour
        GROUP        OLD WAGE       INCREASE      COST PER GROUP
          1           12.30           0.49            46,051
          2           11.95           0.48            62,637
          3           11.30           0.45            52,648
          4           10.05           0.40           119,570
          5            9.50           0.38           165,983
          6            8.95           0.36            61,060
          7            8.40           0.34            43,330
          8            7.90           0.32            24,319


ADDED COST OF THESE CHANGES (INCLUDES ROLL UP):  $657,683
IF YOUR INPUT IS CORRECT, TYPE C & PRESS ENTER KEY.
TO INPUT A DIFFERENT VALUE, PRESS THE ENTER KEY:  C
```

Note: You may give a certain percentage wage increase across-the-board or give each wage group whatever increase you desire. The percentage method was chosen in the example above. Note that fringe costs (roll up) is added to the total costs.

```
COST OF OFFER THIS SESSION $657,683    NOTE:  The cost of your offer
                                       will be subtotalled.

       ***  CONTRACT PROVISION MENU  ***

  * 1 - WAGES FOR 8 GROUPS
  2 - PAID HOLIDAYS
  3 - FUNERAL LEAVE                     An asterisk will be placed
  4 - HEALTH INSURANCE COST             beside each item that has
  5 - CLOTHING ALLOWANCE                been offered to the union.
  6 - PROFIT SHARING
  7 - PENSION BENEFITS
  8 - VACATION
  9 - LONGEVITY PAY
  10 - SHIFT DIFFERENTIAL

  11 - ALL ISSUES FOR THIS OFFER HAVE BEEN ENTERED
  12 - RESTART PROGRAM AT FINANCIAL ISSUES
  13 - RESTART PROGRAM AT THE VERY BEGINNING
  14 - REVIEW THE CURRENT UNION DEMANDS

  INPUT YOUR CHOICE AND PRESS ENTER:  6
```

Note: Profit Sharing plan was selected.

```
Currently the firm does not have a profit sharing plan.  Three years ago the firm had after
tax profits of $990,000; two years ago profits were $1,700,000; and last year $3,064,000.

If the firm made the same profit next year as last, it would cost approximately $30,000 for
each 1% profit the firm paid to its employees ($3,064,000 x 1%).

This $30,000 would give each employee $43 per year ($30,000 divided by 698 employees).

Input the % of the profits you want to give (enter as a whole number):  10

Total cost is $300,000; each employee will get $429 per year.

IF YOUR INPUT IS CORRECT, TYPE C & PRESS ENTER KEY.  TO INPUT A
DIFFERENT VALUE, PRESS THE ENTER KEY?  C
```

COST OF OFFER THIS SESSION $957,683..........   Note that the total has changed to include the cost of profit sharing.

*** CONTRACT PROVISION MENU ***

 * 1 - WAGES FOR 8 GROUPS
2 - PAID HOLIDAYS
3 - FUNERAL LEAVE
4 - HEALTH INSURANCE COST
5 - CLOTHING ALLOWANCE
* 6 - PROFIT SHARING
7 - PENSION BENEFITS
8 - VACATION
9 - LONGEVITY PAY
10 - SHIFT DIFFERENTIAL

11 - ALL ISSUES FOR THIS OFFER HAVE BEEN ENTERED
12 - RESTART PROGRAM AT FINANCIAL ISSUES
13 - RESTART PROGRAM AT THE VERY BEGINNING
14 - REVIEW THE CURRENT UNION DEMANDS

INPUT YOUR CHOICE AND PRESS ENTER: 7

Increase in pension benefits was selected.

PENSION BENEFITS: The current contract reads that employees with 20 years of service are eligible to retire and will receive a annual benefit equal to years of service times 2% of their highest year's base wage. Example: 20 yrs x 2% x $15,000 = $6,000. In this example, increasing the contract formula to 2.2% would give an average of $50 per month increase in pension benefits. The firm currently contributes 5% of the total payroll to the pension plan. The annual cost to the firm is $719,503.

For each additional $50 in monthly retirement income, it will cost an additional $100,000 annually. Enter the desired increase in monthly income for each retired employee (e.g. $30): 50

The monthly income of all retirees will be increased from an average of $350 to $400 at an additional annual cost of $100,000.

IF YOUR INPUT IS CORRECT, TYPE C & PRESS ENTER KEY.
TO INPUT A DIFFERENT VALUE, PRESS THE ENTER KEY:C

HEALTH INSURANCE: The firm Currently pays $90 toward each employee's health insurance premium. This is one half the cost of single coverage.The additional cost of paying the entire single coverage premium would be $490 per year.

How much additional do you want the firm to pay (per employee)? $100

The net annual cost of providing the changes indicated above is $6,000.

To subtotal, type an S and press enter. To exit, type E and Enter. To try a different value, press enter.

*** END OF EXAMPLES ***

INSTRUCTIONS FOR PREPARING STUDENT DISKS

The disk furnished to you may not have the command and control files/programs needed by your brand and model of computer. You will need to prepare a new MASTER disk which can then be used to make as many copies as needed. Follow the instructions below for a two-floppy-disk system. If you have a hard disk, have someone familiar with it prepare your disks.

Turn your computer on with your DOS disk. Eventually you will get an A>. When you do, place a new disk in drive B leaving your DOS disk in drive A and enter as follows after the A>

Format B:/s (and press Enter)

This will format the new disk in drive B and prepare it to be copied onto. The computer will take a minute to do this task and then ask "Format another?" You may respond N (for no). Remove the DOS disk from drive A and place the program disk you received from your instructor in drive A. Input after the A>

Copy *.* b: (and press Enter)   Note: there is a space after copy and a space after the second asterisk

The copy process will take a minute. When finished you will have an A> displayed.

You will now have a new disk in drive B. Remove the original disk from drive A and store it in a cool, dark location. NEVER use this disk for actual use. Keep it as a backup. Place your DOS disk in drive A and type at the A>

Diskcopy A: B: (and press Enter)   Note space after the first colon

The computer will load the diskcopy utility program and then instruct you to place the source disk in drive A and the target disk in drive B. Therefore put your new MASTER disk in drive A and a new disk in drive B; then press Enter. This will copy all the files from your master disk to the new disk and format the new disk at the same time. If you have any trouble with this procedure, get a colleague who has some computer experience to help.

This will prepare disks that are "self-booting." That is, they may be placed in the computer and when the computer is turned on the collective bargaining program will automatically run. If the computer is already on and the A> is showing, simply type MENU and press Enter and the computer will run a menu from which the student can branch. If you are using a computer with a hard disk, transfer control from the C> to the A>. Then place your disk in the A drive and type MENU at the A>

CRITICAL NOTICE:

Many types of (computer) VIRUSES are spreading throughout the world. Use a virus checking program EVERY TIME YOU USE YOUR DISK.